Writing Maniac

Writing Maniac

How I grew up to be a writer
(and you can, too!)

Sheree Fitch

Pembroke Publishers Limited

Pembroke Publishers
538 Hood Road
Markham, Ontario, Canada L3R 3K9
www.pembrokepublishers.com

Distributed in the U.S. by Stenhouse Publishers
477 Congress Street
Portland, ME 04101
www.stenhouse.com

We acknowledge the financial assistance received from the
Government of Canada through the Book Publishing Industry
Development Program (BPIDP) for our publishing activities.

Canadian Cataloguing in Publication Data

Fitch, Sheree
    Writing maniac: how I grew up to be
    a writer (and you can too!)

ISBN 1-55138-121-4

1. Creative writing — Juvenile literature.
2. English language — Composition and
exercises — Juvenile literature. 3. Fitch,
Sheree — Authorship — Juvenile Literature.
I. Title.

PE1408.F46 2000   808'.042   C00-931560-8

Editor: Kat Mototsune
Design: John Zehethofer
Cover Photograph: Paul Darrow

Printed and bound in Canada
9 8 7 6 5 4 3 2 1

Dedication

There are so many people who have been a part of my journey as a writer and who continue to be a part of my heart and my life. This book is dedicated to them:

For my Grade Two teacher, Mrs. Goodwin, who told me that maybe someday I would grow up to be a writer.

For Dr. Mary Lou Stirling and Dr. Fred Cogswell, mentors in the truest sense.

For my father, who told stories.

For my mother, who sang songs.

For my father's English teacher, Nan Geezer, who gave him a love of words and poetry.

For Mary Macchiusi, the publisher of this book, who was patient enough to let me take the time to write, and rewrite, and rewrite.

For my sons, who continue to inspire and teach me.

For all the students and teachers who have taught me that the more you write, the more you must always have a beginner's mind. Thank you for all the letters from young authors, and for all the conferences where I have given workshops.

In memory of Jerry Carty, and for the annual Young Authors Conference held in his honor.

Especially for YOU, dear reader, who are ready to begin. Or begin again. Read and write on!

About Writers

A writer loves words and the world!
Words! Worlds! Words!

A writer will search for words
            reach for words
s t r e t c h words pull words sp lit words s
                                        p
                                i l l   words
play each day with new words
chewable words delicious words twistylipperyslippery words
then say them into the air & onto the page

A writer dreams.
Day dreams night dreams middle of the day dreams sundreams
moon dreams
what will I be someday dreams

A writer smells & tastes & touches & hears & sees sees sees
then looks again —
Writers see an S in a squirrel's tail, hear a poem in the crackle
of fire, discover there are many shades of one color, let music
shimmy inside their bodies, hear the songs that hearts
might sing

A writer feels thinks imagines reads
needs: quiet, noise, adventure, naps
        books, teachers, pencils, paper   erasers!!!!!!

A writer knows they will never know all there is to know about
writing or have all the answers about anything

A writer is not more special or extraordinary than any other
kind of person...BUT

Writing is a kind of magic

A writer is a listener answering the call of that magic...
something as mysterious and wondrous
as the wild west wind or God
or early morning summer skies
& a new-born baby elephant's eyes.

Contents

Dear Reader:

Once upon a time, there was a child who had a dream. The dream was this: When I grow up, I want to be a writer!

The dream came true. I am the writer who was once that child.

Sometimes people ask me how this happened.

I say, **I read a lot and write a lot.**

I say, **I remember and dream.**

I say, **but…I am still learning how to be a writer.**

I say, **so much is still a mystery to me.**

This book is filled with memories, moments in my life that have a lot to do with how and why I grew up to be a writer. There are discoveries and flashes of insight I had as a result of these experiences—each of them is a **WOW**, because it helped me learn more about the **World Of Words**. Then there are letters to you, like this one, containing the real stories behind some of the stories I have written. In the margins and at the end of each of the three sections of the book, you'll find stuff to try: these are ideas that I return to day after day to keep my imagination working and my pencil moving on the page. I have used many of these ideas for the fifteen years I've been doing workshops with writers of all ages. If you come across words you don't know, you might find them in the list of terms at the back of the book. And don't forget to check out my list of books there, too!

I always said I didn't think I would ever write a book about writing, but things happened to change my mind.

Once, after I returned home from giving a workshop in an elementary school, I found a note in my briefcase. It said "Thank-you. When we were writing I could feel the juice in my mind." **Yes!** I thought. That described how writing often feels to me.

Another time, after working with a group of adults, I received a letter that said, "You helped me learn to sing the songs I've hummed so long in my heart. I wish you'd write your stories and ideas in a book."

We all have juice in our mind and songs in our heart and stories we might like to tell. The best advice I ever received was from Dr. Fred Cogswell, a professor and poet. He said, "If you want to be a writer — read and write and read and write and read and write again!"

I hope this book helps you find, like I did, the joys of becoming a Writing Maniac. To find out exactly what I mean by that, well reader, read on. Write on!

sheree

PART ONE

How I Grew Up to Be a Writer

Music & Magic

"Dad, tell me a story…one with your mouth talking." That's how I asked for the poems my father recited. By day he was a Mountie, by night a storyteller! Often, there were no books and no pictures; just the sound of my father's voice.

• • •

Outside the wind is fierce. Snow is sifting against the window-pane, making brittle pebble sounds. I burrow under the covers. For warmth. For safety. Then I hear him. The *thump-galumph-thump* of my father's footsteps. He bursts into the room with his cheeks bulging, his arms flailing, howling like the wind. He is the wind. Then he begins:

> *O wild West Wind, thou breath of Autumn's being,*
> *Thou, from whose unseen presence the leaves dead*
> *Are driven, like ghosts from an enchanter fleeing,*

And on and on and on. At the very end of the poem, his voice booms out the last line:

> *If Winter comes, can Spring be far behind?*

It is over. I know that the storm outside is less frightful, that snow will melt and grass turn green, that bikes will come out and there will be marbles and mud and skipping ropes and… and my mind fills with the thoughts of spring in the middle of a Maritime blizzard.

Long after lights are out for the night, I hear those words collide and boomerang back again. I do not understand all of the words, but I feel their music.

WOW!

Words are a kind of music!

Read a poem out loud.

Read a poem in silence.

Words swirled around our home and took me right out of this world! That's how I learned to love stories and poems.

Besides reciting poems — like the one above, "Ode to the West Wind" by Percy Bysshe Shelley — my father loved to invent stories of his own. When he did, I sometimes got in on it, too. I could decide what a character might say or what would happen next. Sometimes, if I didn't like my father's ending, I could change the ending to one I liked better. When I didn't want to go to sleep, I could keep the story going by saying, "what next?" But eventually the words "lights out for tonight" came every night. It was then, in the silence and shadows of my room, that I kept the story going by myself. I began planning what would happen the next night and realized that anything could happen.

There were so many stories and so many possibilities I discovered in the world of my imagination! My father's words opened up many worlds. He taught me to love the music and the magic of the stories and poems we all tell each other.

Listen for stories your family tells.

WOW!

Words work a kind of magic!

Learn a poem by heart and tell it to someone.

Word Play

My love of poetry is connected to my love of the songs my mother taught me when I was very young. I do not have a very good singing voice, but a poem, for me, is like a spoken-word song. I can hear my mother and me singing together like it just happened this morning.

• • •

There are words
inside of other words.

Uckityboo, I spickety you hiding under the chair
Uckityboo, you sillibee you, I see you ev-er-y-where
Boom! Boom! Boom! Boom!
Uckity boo uckity boo
Sillibee, spickety, uckity BOO!

We're in the kitchen with the sun shining through the window and melting on the tile floor like a square of butter. I am sitting on the green floor, playing the drums on some pots and pans. My mother is doing something at the sink, and she is singing one of my favorite songs — a ditty called "Mairzy Doats."

I want to sing along. I try over and over to get my tongue around the words. My tongue tangles and the more I try, the more mistakes I make. But it's fun. I don't know what the words mean but it's like a secret language, this language of nonsense.

No sense. Ridiculous. Ridiculiculiculous!

Why does something so silly feel so good?

After we're through singing, my mother says it's time to peel potatoes. It's as if I hear the word "potatoes" for the first time. Potatoes. Pot a toes. Pot of toes.

I wonder if I'll have my pot of toes baked or mashed?

Listen for words that
sound like the things
they are:
buzz, murmur,
grumble,
whisper.

When I discovered I could take a word and play with it —stretch it, slide it, bounce it off my tongue and into the air — and find new meaning, I became hooked on words. This is when the word maniac in me was born! Songs and word games with my mother taught me that words are like elastic; stretchy and snappy and changeable. Playing with words is a way of learning to "feel" the music. It was as much fun making sounds with words as it was by making the **clash** and **clang** of pots and pans. Feeling the music could lead me anywhere.

In all the writing I do — plays or poems or stories — the sound of words as they twist off my tongue and the way they sound when they are put together is something I spend a lot of time thinking about. In poetry especially, finding words and sounds within words is important for rhythm and rhyme. Hours and hours and hours of my life have been spent juggling two or three words together until they are the right words in the right places. To a writing maniac, it's a marvelous, mellifluous, magnificent way to spend your time. To a writing maniac, it's all part of a lipslippery adventure with words!

Play the dictionary word-pick game: close your eyes, open the dictionary, find new words. Make a list of your favorites (I call mine my Delicious Word list).

Sing a page of a book.

Words can tickle the tongue.

Play a game of Scrabble.

The Reading Tree

I need a safe place to read and to dream.

My grandmother lived in a house I called the Gingerbread House. The trim around the eaves dipped and swirled like sugar frosting. The house was built on the edge of the edge of the edge of the sea. Or so it seemed to me. There was a hill out back I loved to roll down, flowers almost as tall as I was, and best of all, trees, trees, trees.

The oak tree in front of the house was ancient. Its limbs were many — they reached out and called to me. The leaves whispered secrets. This was the first tree I ever climbed. This was the tree I learned to tie my sneakers in. Inside the first branch was a tiny hollow, a perfect seat where my bottom fit as if the space was made just for me. One day I climbed up into the tree and read a book — all by myself for the first time!

• • •

Find a safe and secret place — indoors and outdoors — to read in, write in, dream in.

I look up from the pages and out from the tree to the ocean. It shines like crinkled foil in the sunlight. There's the smell of salt and seaweed and fish in the air. I hear the bleating of sheep and see them, tiny flecks of sand that freckle the green hill on the other side of the basin. Their baaahs blend into the caws of the gulls. The ocean laps lazily against the rocks. The leaves rustle with every breeze, breathing heavy sighs above my head. Everywhere there is music! Then I return to my book and I am far away again, SEEING, HEARING, SMELLING, SNIFFING, TASTING, and TOUCHING the world inside the book.

Go to the library! It's a safe place for reading and writing.

For me, reading is like the safe and secret place I found in my grandmother's tree. It makes me forget the "real" world and then, when I return to the world I live in, everything seems more alive than before. And, just like reading, writing does that, too.

My favorite writers appeal to my senses when I read. For example, if I read that there was a horrible smell in the air, it doesn't tell me all that much. But if I read **the room smelled like old socks**, I think, "Eeeew!" I'm there, in the world the writer invites me to experience. I think the secret to original writing comes as much from how writers use their senses, their imagination, and their experience as from how they use their words.

Even though reading and writing can shut out the sounds of a noisy room for me, I still like private spaces to read in, write in, dream in. I used to write in bed. Now I have a room in my house. I dream when I'm on long bus trips or sometimes just staring out the kitchen window. I always try to have a pen and paper handy, so I can catch those dreams and get them down. But once I started a poem in a car, where the only paper I had was a napkin. It worked! At least I got a start.

Daydreaming about a story you are working on is a way to keep your imagination flowing. Sometimes, it's hard to turn it off. My children used to know when I was working really hard because I started doing weird things...like putting the dish detergent in the refrigerator! Sometimes the writing maniac can be an absentminded daydreamer.

Writers use their senses!

Look at the world around you. Hear the world around you. Smell the world around you. Feel some object in the world around you. Taste something new today. Start a journal to record your observations.

Word Pictures

My teacher was at the chalkboard, writing something. "Write this in your notebook," she told us, so I did. I printed:

> *The fog comes*
> *on little cat feet*
>
> *It sits looking*
> *over city and harbor*
> *on silent haunches*
> *and then moves on*
>
> *– Carl Sandburg*

A writer makes surprise connections!

• • •

I stare at the words of "Fog" and something strange begins to happen. The page seems to glow. The words seem to wriggle across it. It's like I can see underneath the page or right through it into some other world. I see how fog moves like a cat. *Yes!* I think to myself: *it's just like that, isn't it?* Only I never would have thought of it that way. Until now.

"This," says the teacher, "is a poem. The poet makes a comparison between a cat and fog. These are two very different things and he finds a connection between them. This is a figure of speech called a metaphor."

Metaphor. I feel like someone handed me a magic word.

Go on a Metaphor Treasure Hunt. Go outside and see how many things are different from, but connect to other things.

Many writers would say they had a moment like this that changed their lives forever. I would never see fog again without thinking of the Carl Sandburg poem. Even today, when I watch my cat Daisy out in the yard sitting on her haunches, I think of the poem.

This is what ALL writing is about: making connections. Seeing how one thing is like another thing, or different from it. Looking at the world and what's in it in new ways. When I discovered that a poem could say so much in so few words, I wanted to know more!

Poetry uses figures of speech, like metaphor. From that day, I understood what that was! Metaphors help you see underneath the page to what the words mean. Metaphors make pictures in your mind — so that's what a metaphor's for! Yet there are so many other figures of speech: there is simile, for example, and alliteration and consonance, and imagery, and — a really hard one to spell — onomatopoeia. Understanding metaphor was just the beginning of my curiosity about how writers write. I learned that there are all kinds of poems — long poems and short poems, poems that rhyme and those that don't, story poems like ballads, poems that have a certain form like haiku and sonnet.

I discovered something else, too. When you are open to discovering metaphor, life can never ever be boring! It is like a game of I Spy — I spy with my little eye something that reminds me of something else. Then it's like a game of connect the dots. You see that everything is connected. It's awesome! It's fun!

Draw a picture you find in a poem.

A metaphor compares and connects two things that are very very different.

Name Game

If I try, and if I have patience, I can write!

My Grade Two teacher was a kind, merry woman named Mrs. Goodwin. Good. Win. Even her name made me happy. She read stories out loud to us. She was the teacher who gave me the gift of the fog poem and explained about metaphor. She was the one who gave me lots of magic words. And she was the one who gave me a challenge that changed my life!

• • •

"Okay, class, we are all going to write poems," Mrs. Goodwin says. Music to my ears!

"But we don't know what to write about," someone says.

Tell someone a story to make them smile.

"Nonsense," says our teacher. "How do you know until you try? Besides, you can write about anything! The sun. A shoelace. Your name. But write!"

So I do. I cross out and erase many times until I get this:

> I'm an itchy Fitch
> I live in a ditch
> I'm not very rich
> I look like a witch
> Sometimes, I itch.
> Itchy, twitchy, witchy Fitch.

Tell a ghost story.

I show it to Mrs. Goodwin. "Yes!" she says, smiling. "This is a poem, a kind of poem called a nonsense poem. A sort of tongue-twister."

She prints it on the board and the whole class reads it. Everybody laughs!

A few weeks after my first poem was written, Mrs. Goodwin thumbtacked my poem on a felt panel for our class display at the school fair. In a way, it was like my first published poem! I watched as other students and parents read it and smiled and showed it to friends. I told Mrs. Goodwin how excited I was, seeing what happened when people read something I wrote.

"I know what I want," I said. "I want to grow up and be a writer and make poems and stories that make people smile!"

"I know you can do it!" said Mrs. Goodwin. All that year and the next (she was my Grade Three teacher too) I wrote poems for Mrs. Goodwin. She gave them back with lots of notes about how I could make them better. This is when I learned that a writing maniac needs a lot of patience. . .and erasers!

Dream of something
you want to do.
See it in your mind.
Play it like a movie
over and over.
Imagine ways to
make your
dream come true.
Listen for words of
encouragement
around you.

Words have
the power to make
people smile.
Or cry. Or think.
Or be afraid!

Hiding My Dream

To do what you really want to do sometimes makes you feel different and alone.

In high school, I still dreamed of being a writer. I didn't dare tell anyone and kept all my writing secret. My friends cared mostly about sports, and thought that I was just like they were. I loved sports, but I had another side to me, too! One day, I saw a notice that a teacher was starting a creative writing club for students who loved to write. I was excited but…could I find the courage to go?

· · ·

Look in the mirror. Pretend the person in the mirror is speaking, telling you what he or she sees. (Write it down.)

It's four o'clock. Most of my friends are in the cafeteria waiting for soccer or basketball practice to begin. I have made arrangements with my coach to skip practice one day a week. I have to walk by everyone to get to creative writing class. I hold my breath. I don't want any of them to ask me where I am going. I do not want any of my friends to know about my dream of becoming a writer. "Artsy fartsy" — that's what they call the people who join clubs like this. I know they will make fun of me.

"Hey, where ya going, Fitch?" Just as I feared.

"Um…detention," I reply and make a face. They all laugh.

I can't believe it! I just told a lie because I didn't have courage to tell them the truth.

I leave the cafeteria, still shaking. Too soon, I'm at the classroom with the sign, Creative Writing Club. I go in. There are only six other people and the teacher. I am the only grade ten student.

There are always other people as different and alone as you.

"Well," says Mrs. Blanchett, "let's start writing. Write about why you are here."

I want to write that I don't have a clue. I want to write that it's because I am weird. But I begin by writing that, ever since I was in grade two, I wanted to be a writer.

Imagine! I told a little lie that day because I was ashamed of what I had been dreaming about. Why couldn't I say, "I'm on my way to a creative writing club"? Well, in the neighborhood I lived in there were no writers, or at least no people I knew were writers. By the time I was in high school, I thought my dream was sort of silly, like wanting to be a rock-and-roll star. I was afraid of being laughed at. I wanted to fit in with my crowd. Back then, there were no author visits to schools, and being a writer seemed as fantastic an idea as going to the moon. So I kept it from almost everyone. But guess what! People do grow up to be rock-and-roll stars and astronauts and writers! They might even come from neighborhoods just like the one you live in.

Now that I'm older, I realize that almost everyone feels different and alone at times — no matter what they do or dream of doing. Now I realize that my friends might have understood my dream, or even thought it was cool! And, if they did make fun of me for my dream, maybe they were not true friends.

In that writing class and the one I took a few years later, I met a lot of people who shared the writing dream. I discovered that there are all kinds of people who were writing maniacs just like me.

But every writing maniac — just like every person — is different. I learned, and I am still learning, that difference is not something to be ashamed of or afraid of. It truly is what makes us human beings.

Ask for an author visit to your school. It doesn't have to be a book author: journalists, playwrights, poets, songwriters — they're all writers! Start a book club at school or with your friends.

Ask your parents, older brothers or sisters, or other adults if they ever felt different or embarrassed or alone because of what they liked to do or had to do.

Terrific Teachers

Read and write about an author you like.

Twenty-three years after I wrote my first poem, I went to a bookstore to sign books. My first published book! I kept holding the book in my hands, flipping through the pages — *Toes in my Nose*, a real book with my name on the cover and Molly Lamb Bobak's funky and fun artwork. I couldn't believe it. But I always remembered that Mrs. Goodwin told me I could do it. I tried. Now, it was happening!

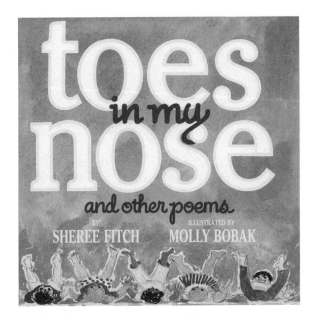

Every writer needs a someone who believes in them and helps them with their writing.

• • •

In the bookstore, there is a line-up of people waiting to get books autographed. I keep signing my name and saying "thank you." I am really nervous. I don't even look at the people. Then someone puts a book in front of me, a woman who looks familiar. She says, "Sheree, maybe you could write your name on my forehead."

What? I wonder. Then I look again at the woman pointing to her forehead. "Mrs. Goodwin!" I shriek. I jump up and hug her.

It turns into quite a reunion, with happy tears and Kleenex and everything. It has been almost twenty years since the last time I saw her.

She says she still has poems I wrote in her class. She even quotes from them. It's like she knew all along that I would be a writer. I recite "Itchy Fitch." I proudly sign my name in the copy of my first book that I give to her.

You have to know the rules before you break the rules.

It was a very long journey from my first writing class in high school to that day at the book store. Teachers and family were the most important part of that journey.

After high school, the next writing class I took was at the Maritime Writer's Workshop. I was as nervous as ever about taking the course, but it changed my life. I met and listened to other real writers. Real people. Nancy Bauer, Bill Bauer, Ann Copeland, W.D. Valgardson, David Adams Richards. They lived! They wrote! If they could do it, could I?

When you are writing, use your senses, your imagination and your experience, and think about each word you use.

At that workshop, I met Dr. Fred Cogswell, a poet and translator who taught English at university. Fred encouraged me to keep writing. He gave me lots of books of poetry because he always said this: you have to know the rules before you break the rules. One day, Fred brought me the book **Alligator Pie**, by Dennis Lee. **Wow!** I thought. **You can live in Canada and be a writer of nonsense, the kind of poetry I loved the most!** Even with all this encouragement I might have given up. I got a few poems published, but most of my writing was rejected.

Then, another important teacher came into my life. My mother was a secretary at the University of New Brunswick, and showed my poems to Mary-Lou Stirling, a professor of education there. Dr. Stirling became like a fairy godmother and a friend all rolled into one. The very first time I met her, she said to me, "Sheree **when** you have your book published, elementary school children will love it and teachers will use it to teach." She said **when** not if. She insisted I send my poems out again and again. Along with Fred, she also inspired me to go to university.

My writing dream had begun to come true. I was writing and telling stories and poems to students. I remember thinking that it didn't matter if I ever had a book published, because I found people who wanted to listen. I believed that until the day I got the phone call — the editor at Doubleday told me they were publishing my first book. At first I thought someone was playing a joke on me! Then I whooped and hollered. I laughed. I cried. I called my mother and father, my children, Fred, and Mary Lou — in that order.

Six months after my reunion with Mrs. Goodwin, I gave a reading in a library. When it was over, a woman came up to me. "I'm Nan," she said. "Nan Geezer." I couldn't believe it. She was my father's high school English teacher, the one who had taught him all the poems he used to recite to me! Imagine — in some wonderful, magical way, what was happening to me was because of a great teacher and lover of words I had never met!

- Sharpen your senses with this fill-in-the blank exercise (I've given you some examples to get you started):

  - As red as (tomato sauce)_____
  - As cold as (a polar bear's nose) _____
  - As hot as (sand in the Sahara)_____
  - As dark as (the mouth of a killer whale)_____
  - As blue as_____
  - As soft as_____
  - As hard as_____
  - As sour as _____
  - As sharp as _____
  - As round as_____
  - A slippery as_____

- Return to this list as often as you want and add to it, too.

- Write for five minutes using every one of your five senses. Topic suggestions: eating breakfast, going camping, going to the mall.

- Pick a letter from the alphabet. On your mark, get set, go! For one minute, write down all the words you can think of that begin with that letter. Stop! Read the list. It's the beginning of a tongue-twister poem or paragraph.

- Make a list of ten favorite books. Make notes of what you think makes great writing.

- Define a strong emotion using metaphor.

  Examples: Anger is a red jagged scar
  Loneliness is a phone that never rings
  Hunger is a grand canyon belly
  Fear is walking into mouth of an
  abandoned mine
  Love is holding a baby lamb in your arms.

- Define strong emotion using a simile.

  Examples: When I'm angry, I feel like a boiling pot of potatoes. She was so afraid her kneebones knocked together like chattering teeth.

- Write a word picture.

  Example: A moving van pulls up to my best friend's house.

  Now test it! Ask someone to tell you what emotion they feel when they read it.

- Make up a Metaphor Riddle.

  Example: What do shoes, tires, and mothers have in common? They can all get worn out!

- Write an unrhymed poem about rain modeled on Carl Sandburg's "Fog":

  > The rain _____
  >
  > _____ _____ _____ _____
  >
  > It _____ _____
  >
  > _____ _____
  >
  > And then _____ _____

- Now try writing poems about the snow, a cloud, the sun, a star, the moon.

- Write a Word Portrait. From a list of people who are important in your life, choose one to write a paragraph about. Remember to use your senses!

  Example: Mrs. Goodwin smelled like chalk dust and lilies. When she walked by my desk, her dresses made whispery sounds.

- Write a poem playing and rhyming with the sound of your name.

PART TWO

Ideas Here, There, and Everywhere

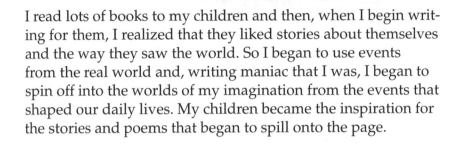
In The Everyday World

WOW!

Looking through
another's eyes is
necessary for
a writer.

I read lots of books to my children and then, when I begin writing for them, I realized that they liked stories about themselves and the way they saw the world. So I began to use events from the real world and, writing maniac that I was, I began to spin off into the worlds of my imagination from the events that shaped our daily lives. My children became the inspiration for the stories and poems that began to spill onto the page.

• • •

Jordan, my oldest son, is about three years old. After his bath, he refuses to get out of the tub until all the water drains away. His brown eyes are as wide as pie plates, and are glued to the swirl of water as it gupples down the drain.

"Look at that little man down there!" he shrieks and points.

"What?" I think maybe one of his toys is caught in the drain.

"That little man down there," he repeats. I look again.

"There's no little man down there," I start to say but then stop. Suddenly, I remember! I know exactly what he's talking about. That little whirlpool thingie fascinated me when I was young, too. I would stare at it and wonder: if I got my toe stuck would I be sucked right down there, just like that little sliver of soap that swiveled and swirled and disappeared?

I used to imagine a whole universe underneath our world,

WOW!

Remembering is an
important part
of writing.

tiny creatures whom I had never met, living there. They lived in boats, I figured. I had questions. Did they sneak up to our world when we weren't looking? What language did they speak? What did they do each time the water gushed down upon them on its way to the ocean? (I pictured the bathtub water ending up in the ocean.) So I play along with Jordan.

"Right," I say, "that little man down there."

Jordan nods, excited that I get it.

"What do you think we should call him?" I ask.

"That's easy," he says. "He lives in the plug, so his name is Mr. Blug."

"Mr. Blug! Of course," I laugh.

Blug in the Plug in the Tub

At the end of my bath
When I pull out the plug
There's a monster down there
We call The Blug!!!

There's a blug in the plug in the tub
It gurgles and swirls and rumbles
It gobbles up toys
With thunderous noise
It burps and it growls and it grumbles
Well the blug in the plug in the tub
I have never really seen
But I've heard it roar
By the bathroom door
And in the washing machine

The blug in the plug and the tub
The blug in the plug in the tub
Blug in the plug
Blug in the tub
Glug, glug, glug, glug.

Imagination is fun, playful, and makes a kind of magical world. If you don't use it, you might lose it!

Sometimes we speak
in rhyme.

I'm happy. I have two wonderful, healthy children. Dustin, Jordan's new baby brother, is playing on a blanket on the floor. Jordan is playing quietly beside him.

Dustin is doing what little babies often do, sticking his feet in his mouth.

"Dustin!" says Jordan, "that's disgusting! And if you're not careful," he teases, tickling the bottom of his little brother's feet, "You just might stick your toes in your nose!"

"Toes in your nose!" I shout, "Toes in my nose!"

It's the beginning of a poem!

WOW!

You can hear poems
all around!

Toes in my Nose

I stuck my toes
In my nose
And I couldn't get them out.
It looked a little strange
And people began to shout
"Why would you ever?
My goodness—I never!"
They got in a terrible snit
It's simple, I said
As they put me to bed
I just wanted to see
If they fit.

. . .

Jordan bounces into the kitchen. "I'm hungry!" he announces, "and I'm going to make my own peanut butter sandwich. All by myself!"

"Sure," I say. I help him push a chair to the counter. He gets out the peanut butter and the bread and starts to make his sandwich.

"I'll make a peanut butter and honey sandwich," he decides. I open the honey jar and pass it to him.

Then Jordan gets into trouble. Sticky trouble. He starts to spread the honey and it globs onto the countertop, his hands, even his face — everywhere except the bread. He gets down from the chair, stomps his foot on the floor, and says, "Mum, how do you get the honey from the bottle to the bread?"

"Hmm. How do you get the honey from the bottle to the bread?" I repeat. I begin to snap my fingers to the rhythm. I run to get a piece of paper. I begin to write until Jordan says, "Mum! Help!" Oops! He's still in sticky trouble.

Spreading Honey

How do you get the honey
From the bottle to the bread
Without the bottle slipping
Honey dripping
On your head?

How do you get the honey
From the bread to your tummy?
It's yicky and it's sticky
But it's sweet and it's yummy.

Well, how do you get the honey
From the bottle to the bread
Without the bottle slipping
Honey dripping
On your head?

You whirl it
You twirl it
You lick it up quick
Then you ask your mommy
For a honey stick.

THAT'S how you get the honey
From the bottle to the bread
Without the bottle slipping
Honey dripping on your head.

• • •

Jordan is already in the tub and I pick up his jeans where he's left them — on his bedroom floor again. A pile of rocks falls out of his pockets onto the floor. I holler out to him, "Jordan, a pocketful of rocks! A pocket full of rocks. What are you going to do with a pocket full of rocks?"

"Hey, Mum, that sounds like one of your poems!" he sings back out. Now he's becoming a poetry maniac, too!

You can make others
hear poems
all around.

Pocketful of Rocks

A pocketful of rocks
A pocketful of rocks
What do you do
With a pocketful of rocks?

Well, you put those rocks
In your brother's blue socks
And then you watch him walk
With his socks
Full of rocks.

A pocketful of rocks
A pocketful of rocks
That's what you do
With a pocketful of rocks.

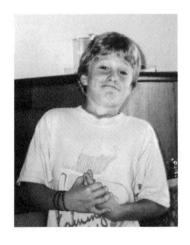

A sentence someone
speaks can be the
first line of a poem.

• • •

Dustin is trying and trying and trying to say the word "spaghetti." But he can't…. He says "pasketii" instead. I tell Dustin I have a word that tangles my tongue, too!

"What is it, Mum?"

"Cinnamon," I say. Or try to. I can't. I say "cimanom" or "synanim." So I start repeating it to myself. Cinnamon. Cinnamon. I take out a piece of chalk. I write it on the blackboard in my kitchen. Cinnamon.

"Sin a min," I say. "Swimmin' in," I say. "Swimmin' in cinnamon," I say. Put your Mama in, Cinnamon. Cinnamon's mama is swimmin' in Cinnamon. Mama is grinnin' and swimmin' in cinnamon.

Maybe I should try to write about the word. By the time I'm finished, I will never make a mistake with it again!

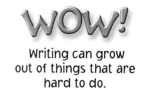

Writing can grow out of things that are hard to do.

Zelba Zinnamon

Zelba Zinnamon she loved cinnamon
She loved cinnamon cake
Zelba Zinnamon
Nose full of cinnamon
Got a belly ache
Then Zelba Zinnamon
Sniffed the cinnamon
Got her nose all red
Zelba Zinnamon
Nose full of cinnamon
Had to go to bed.

Okay! I admit it! By then, the writing maniac was on the loose big time! All of these stories really happened, and started ideas for the poems published in **Toes in my Nose**. They show how situations from everyday life, sprinkled with imagination and lots of wordplay, can inspire a poem. But...not one of those poems came with the "first burst" of the idea. I wrote and crossed out, wrote and crossed out, wrote and erased many, many times. And that goes for every poem, even one as small as "A Pocketful of Rocks."

After I had visited a Grade Two class in St. Stephen, New Brunswick, I got a letter from a girl named Deana Jay.

> Dear Sheree Fitch:
> Here is a poem for you.
> A pocketful of ants, a pocketful of ants
> What do you do, with a pocketful of ants?
> Well, you put those ants
> In your brother's white pants
> Then you watch him do
> The boogie-woogie dance
> That's what you do, with a pocketful of ants!

She said she only did two drafts. I liked her poem better than mine!

So when I say that I believe you can make a poem or story out of just about anything when you are a writing maniac, I mean it! You can even twist a poem of someone else's around. Keep open for ideas — it's an exciting way to go into each day.

WOW!

What you end up with might be a long way from where you started!

In Your Dreams!

The boys and I once lived in a little, crooked, yellow house in Fredericton, New Brunswick. We loved the house even though it wasn't ours. The owner let me paint the kitchen cupboards happy blue and turquoise. Pinned on the walls and taped to the refrigerator were pictures of dragons and other characters from my books that had been painted by students. The ceilings were low and the house sometimes felt crowded, especially as the boys were getting taller and taller. In fact, both my boys had dreams of playing basketball in the NBA. Luckily for us, our landlord put up a basketball net in the driveway — and that house, that kitchen, a basketball, and a dream had a lasting effect on our lives.

Sounds of the world around you, not just the sound of words, can begin ideas for stories or poems.

•   •   •

The boys are outside playing basketball before lesson time begins. I'm clearing the supper chaos away and doing the dishes. I'm tired and grumpy. I fill the sink with sudsy water and begin to work. I love the warm water on my hands! The window is open and I start to really listen to the *thump thump thwang* of the basketball as it hits the pavement and then the backboard. I can even hear the slick swishiness of the ball going through the hoop: *thump swish, thump thump thwang, thump thwang thump thump thump swish*. There is a music there, I think. A rhythm. I begin to do a little jig at the sink in time to the basketball *thumpthwang* and *swish* and

There Were Monkeys in my Kitchen!

Sheree Fitch   Marc Mongeau

I start to feel a whole lot better. I will have to write a thwang swish thump kind of basketball poem some time. Hmm. I start to daydream the way I do when I get an idea.

THUMP THUMP THUMP. The thumps get louder all of a sudden and, before I know it, both boys are in the kitchen out of breath and still bouncing the basketball. "Mum could we have a drink of water?" *THUMP! THUMP THUMP!* The whole kitchen floor shakes and the dishes rattle in the cupboard. I do what I think any mother would do.

"You two monkeys get those basketballs out of the kitchen right this minute!" I say as I turn on the tap for water.

"We're not monkeys, Mum!" they say.

"Oh, yes you are. There are monkeys in my kitchen, now be gone!" We all laugh and they thump back out the door. That was that. Or so I thought.

• • •

A few months later I am out of town working in schools as a visiting author. I've been gone a week, and now I am going to stay for the weekend to give more workshops to adults interested in writing. But I miss my boys. Before I go to sleep, I think about them and about the basketball game I'm going to miss the next day. I fall asleep with all this on my mind. In the middle of the night I wake up, sit up in bed, and say out loud in the dark:

> There were monkeys in my kitchen
> They were climbing up the walls
> They were dancing on the ceiling
> They were bouncing basketballs.

Four lines come tumbling out of my mouth into the room before I am fully awake. Talk about talking in your sleep! I scribble the lines down in the notebook beside my bed. The next morning, I read the lines over. Mmm. This could be the beginning of a poem for sure. Mmm.

WOW!

Real life plus dreams plus imagination can be the source of a story.

There is so much we do not know about how our imaginations work. The importance of dream to our real lives is mysterious and fascinating. Legends and myths are often filled with dreams. Poets and painters use their dreams as part of the work they create.

I have always had very vivid dreams that seem real. Whenever I am really stuck writing a story or book or play, I think about it before I go to sleep. Sometimes, the next day, I know where to go with the writing! Other times, I go for a walk and I play the story like a movie or dream I am having in my head. Then I can hardly wait to get home and turn the daydream into words on the page. The poem that came from daydreaming and dreaming became a book called — what else? — **There Were Monkeys in my Kitchen!**

Have you ever had a dream about someone you know, but they are someone else at the same time? If you're a writing maniac, you get to play with characters just like your dreaming mind does. In the monkey book, my sons are there, and there are other real people too. My sister is Leanne Jane the Mountie, and in real life she is a police officer. My father was a Mountie when I was growing up and he was never allowed to chew gum in his uniform; so in this book, he gets to blow bubbles! And the monkey called Deborah Louise is really my best friend. As a writer, you can change your best friends into monkeys and put them in a story!

P.S. When I went to Africa I met a boy who said, "Sheree Fitch, we really did have monkeys in our kitchen and it wasn't funny at all!"

Many ideas need time before they are written.

☀ THE WRITE STUFF

- Look for magic in ordinary things.

- Create a world of creatures, and name them. Draw a map of where they live. Write about them; invent words for them to say.

- Write using something somebody says to you as a way to begin.

- Write using this model:

> A pocketful of _____
> A pocketful of _____
> What do you do
> With a pocketful of _____?
> Well you put those _____
> _____.
> That's what you do
> With a pocketful of _____!

- Write for five minutes about something you collect. If you do not collect anything, make it an imaginary list. Listen to the sounds in each word. Arrange the words in lines. You have an unrhymed poem!

- List words that are hard to say and play with the sound in them.

- Write a silly sentence using as many Z words as you can.

- Keep a dream journal and record things in your dreams — even the scary things.

- Make a collage about the next dream you remember by cutting out pictures from magazines and pasting them on a poster or piece of bristol board.

- Write a story where a character has a strange dream. Describe every detail of the dream no matter how weird. In fact, make it as weird and wild as you can.

- Listen for the music in the world around you. Some examples: the ticking of the clock, the click of a dog's toenails on the floor, the calling of crows, the rain on the roof. Write words to that music.

- Write about a sport you like. Or don't like.

- Make a list of verbs that describe movement. Some examples: leap, straddle, cartwheel, bounce, scramble.

- Write about some kind of animal ending up where no animals usually are. Some examples: pandas in the swimming pool, kangaroos in the grocery store, hippos at a hockey game.

- Pick a country on the map, and do some research on that country. Write about what you think it would be like to visit that country, or live in that country.

PART THREE

Being a Writing Maniac

Dancing With Dragons

I decided to go to university to study English because I knew there was so much about writing I needed to learn. One way to do that was to study the great writers and their works. I went to St. Thomas University in Fredericton, New Brunswick, and my professors made those four years some of the most wonderful of my life. They challenged and encouraged, they supported and listened. I had children and had a lot to juggle — housework, homework, and motherhood. When Jordan had a day off school, he even went to class with me. He loved to tease me: "Mum, no television until after your homework is done!"

• • •

I'm doing homework late one night, after the boys have gone to bed. I am very sleepy, trying to stay awake and read a poem to prepare for class the next day. The poem is "The Eve of St. Agnes" by John Keats. It's a long, long poem and I love it. But still, I think I'm nodding off to sleep when I read these words:

Writers inspire other writers.

> She hurried at his words, beset with fears
> For there were sleeping dragons all around,
> At glaring watch, perhaps, with ready spears—
> Down the wide stairs a darkling way they found—
> In all the house was heard no human sound.

Listen to a piece
of instrumental music
(without words) that
inspires you. What
story or dream does
it tell you?

I shiver. Outside my window, the dark seems suddenly darker. *For there were sleeping dragons all around.* Wow! Great line. I love the music in it, but I also love the sense of danger. I write the line down on a piece of paper. Sounds like the beginning of a poem or story, I think, but I wonder if you can borrow a line from another writer?

Ten minutes later after I read that line, Dustin wakes up and starts calling for me. When I reach his bedside, he says he had a bad dream and "there were sharks all around." It's like an echo of the Keats line.

I give him a drink of water and wait until he settles back down. I go downstairs, back to my homework. Except I'm not concentrating on the homework. My brain is in rewind. When I was small and woke up from a bad dream, I wanted to go downstairs but I was too afraid of the dark. Just like Dustin, I imagined there was something in the dark that could hurt me. I remember lying in bed, my eyes wide open, watching shadows dance about my room.

I wrote down one line. . . **There are sharks in the dark.** Then, I looked over at the line from Keats about the dragons, and I started writing. I began with **SHH! SHH! There are sleeping dragons all around...** and the whole story flashed in front of my mind. I began writing "Sleeping Dragons All Around" that night, but it took me more than two years to finish it.

Sometimes, classes send me poems they have made about their own special dragons. Dragons that play Nintendo, that play basketball, that smell like rotten oranges. What imagination I have seen in these poems and pictures! The writers tell me that my book inspired their writing. I think that the poet John Keats, who inspired me, might be laughing to think that after more than a hundred years one of his lines would start a children's book and that others would write about those dragons, too!

To me, this is another way writing connects us to each other — even the writers who are no longer with us. It shows me how powerful the written word really is. The thought that writing maniacs can give energy to each other's creative thoughts over time and space, even if we never meet, is magical to me. That's also one of the reasons I still read so much, even things that were written way before I was born.

Look at a photo or picture that inspires you. What story does it tell you?

Read a book by a dead writer.

Read a book by a writer from another country.

Read a biography of a a writer you like.

Bumper Car Theory of the Universe

When I lived in Fredericton, every September, I looked forward to the week that school began. That same week, there was an event that was more exciting than going back to school! It was the Fredericton Exhibition. Like any fair, it had cotton candy and rides and animals and contests and…well, it was amazing! It still is. I love the bumper cars!

Writing doesn't have to be in a straight line on a page!

• • •

Dustin and I are waiting in the long line, waiting for our ride on the bumper cars. I do not like waiting! I remember something my writing teacher told me: You don't have to just write about things you like; you can write about something you don't like, too. So I start paying attention.

I notice something. In line, everyone is laughing and talking. Then, as soon as they get into their bumper cars, the looks on their faces change. It's safe and fun, but they are really trying hard to ram each other good! When the ride is over, they wave to each other and say good-bye. People are so happy. For just a second I giggle to myself: What if everyone had bumper cars

in their backyard? Wouldn't the whole world be a whole lot happier? What a safe way to get out frustration!

My mind starts to wander. There are poems everywhere at the Ex! I sniff (a french-fry smell), I hear (a train-track clatter), I see (zigzag shapes everywhere). I touch the cotton candy and think of a pink, sticky cloud. I take in all the sights and sounds and shapes around me.

When I get home from the Ex, I'm dizzy with excitement. I start out with a line about standing in line:

> Standing in line
>> all the little kids whine

Then, I write the poem shaped like a line, with the words being the people.

Next, I begin to write a bumper-car poem and try to make the poem match the way the bumper cars start off slowly and then speed up.

Next, I have an idea for the rollercoaster and I'm off! I know I have an idea for a whole book — a book that would become *Merry-Go-Day*.

Read a book with a cover you don't like.

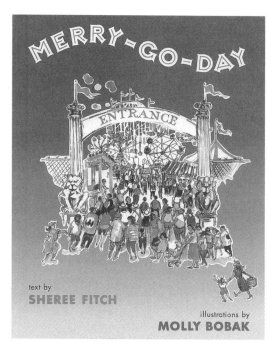

MERRY-GO-DAY

ENTRANCE

text by
SHEREE FITCH

illustrations by
MOLLY BOBAK

WOW!

Things we don't like can inspire us to write, too!

I learned a lot that day at the fair. I learned about energy— how you could take all the muddle and confusion of a place and even things you don't like and use that in your writing. I learned how, just when I was getting really frustrated with standing in line, I could get curious instead. I could see this another chance to be a writing maniac! The Ex became even more thrilling!

When poems are placed on the page in a shape —like the poem I wrote in the shape of a line of people — they are called concrete poems. But the words you choose to use also give shape and energy to your writing. All the different parts of speech — nouns, pronouns, verbs, adjectives, and adverbs — are there to help you get movement and what you feel from all your senses into your writing, so the reader can get it back out!

Of all my books, **Merry-Go-Day** is the one that hasn't been as "popular" as some of the others. That means it did not sell as many. It's important to listen to the opinions of people you respect, and readers often show that respect by buying the book. How can a book be a book if it doesn't get read? How can a poem be a poem if it doesn't get heard? But there are other times, when you really feel you have stretched and done your very best in your writing. Not every one will know this. But you will! Guess what — I think some of my best poems are in **Merry-Go-Day**! Trust your own feelings, too.

In **Merry-Go-Day**, a girl tries to win a purple parrot and doesn't. Sometimes people tell me this surprises them. Sometimes, they ask me why it isn't a happy ending. Hmm. It is to me. In the end, the girl hears fireworks and looks out her bedroom window. She says,

> There's my parrot! Purple parrot!
> In a blaze across the sky,
> I'll be back next year, I whisper
> This is goodnight but not good-bye.

She knows the Ex will be back! Besides, we don't always get what we want when we want it, right? I never won the purple parrot when I was little. So, a writer can use their imagination OR be truthful to their own experience. Or both!

Invent words for sounds. Some examples: **goosh goosh** for stepping in mud, **shkewp** for sucking through a straw in an almost empty glass.

A Purple Sort of Girl

When someone asks a good question, you can get a new idea!

Everyone has a favorite color. I like blues and purples. When I was in high school, I was a real purple maniac! My bedroom was pink and purple. I had purple posters on the wall. I had a purple coat. I listened to a music group called Deep Purple! Besides the color, I loved the ripple of the *-urple* sound, the tickle of my tongue when I said those letters. One day, a purple girl paid me a visit!

Mabel Murple

Mabel Murple's house was purple
So was Mabel's hair
Mabel Murple's cat was purple
Purple everywhere!

Mabel Murple's bike was purple
So were Mabel's ears
When Mabel Murple cried
She cried terrible purple tears.

Start a Color Word Collection. Look in paint stores, at nail polish and lipstick names, at car colors, in fashion magazines. Especially look out your back door!

• • •

It's question-and-answer period in a Grade Two classroom. A little girl puts up her hand. "Why is Mabel Murple crying?"

Ahhhh! I don't have an answer!

"I don't know," I say.

"Well," said the girl, "It wasn't very nice of you to leave her in that book crying."

"No it wasn't," I agree, "especially without even knowing why she was crying!"

"What if you wrote more Mabel Murple poems?" the girl suggests.

"What if I did?" I agree.

What if there was a whole purple world? Aha! I feel the purple maniac and the writing maniac in me at work — together!

I realized that I hadn't finished with Mabel Murple and, before I had a chance to blink, I started getting Mabel Murple poems from students! It seemed as if Mabel Murple herself came to life and told me that she didn't want to be left crying. She wanted to have a good time, too! She wanted a book of her very own.

One day I asked myself this question again —**what if** there was a purple planet with purple people on it? I wrote down that sentence. That sentence became the first line of the book. An ordinary girl imagines a purple world. The book is a series of tongue-twisters showing Mabel and all the wacky, topsy-turvy purple things she does. Color and sound helped me create a whole universe! The words **what if** got my imagination going!

Through Mabel Murple, I learned that characters can take on a life of their own when you start "listening" to them. Because of teachers and students, I learned that books can become the starting point for real-life fun. I often receive great poems about Gertrude Green from classes who have modeled their poetry after the character that Mabel meets at the end of the book.

A few years ago, when I went to visit St. Gerard's school in Grande Prairie, Alberta, classes decorated a whole room like Mabel Murple's world. Everyone was dressed in purple, even the teachers! There were purple flowers on a table, sheets of purple tissue paper over the window, and a purple light over a special seat, just like Mabel's bed in the book. That's where I sat to do my readings. It was amazing. I felt like I was Mabel Murple that day!

Asking **what if** can be the beginning of a poem or story or play!

Have a party and invite your friends to dress as their favorite book character!

Think Again

If we think again, sometimes we see something in a different way.

My father used to say to us, "Whenever you think you have thought of everything, think again!" He had a head full of quotes for every occasion and, like most parents, he used every chance he got to give us good advice. When I became a parent, I told my children to "think again" too. Sometimes, the results were amazing.

• • •

The boys and I are in a car with friends at the top of a hill. "Look, there's rain down there," someone says, "We're dry and they're wet! Neat!"

Then everyone starts telling their favorite stories about rain.

"I was caught in a hail storm," says Billy. "Once I was on one side of the street and it was raining on the other."

Charlotte, our driver, says suddenly, "You won't believe this but it's true. Once I stood right where the rainbow ended. It was like I could almost reach up and touch it."

Wow! Then, everyone talks at once. "Was there…?"

Charlotte laughs. "That's what everyone asks," she says. "I'm sorry to have to tell you, but no. There is no pot of gold at the end of the rainbow."

We are all quiet. We liked being able to believe in the story of the pot of gold, and are a bit sad to have that possibility taken away. About fifteen minutes later, just as we are turning in the driveway, Dustin, who is six, leans forward. "But Charlotte," he says seriously, "how do you know you weren't at the beginning of the rainbow?"

Everyone laughs but Charlotte. "Dustin, you're right! No one has ever thought of that before!"

We are relieved! There is still the possibility of that pot of gold waiting for everyone!

List five things most important to you in your life now. If you were three years old, what would they be? What about if you were sixteen? Forty? Eighty?

Inside-up and downside-out! How do we look at things? My son Dustin was the youngest in the car that day, but he showed me how "big" a thinker he was. He showed us all how an ending can be a beginning. A writer's mind must be able to twist things and turn them and discover new ways of looking!

Not long after this happened, we were in a car driving into a city. As we entered the city, we saw a series of smoke stacks with smoke billowing out. Yuck! Pollution, I thought. "Look Mummy, cloud-makers!" said Dustin, excited. It was as if he finally discovered how clouds were made. He thought it was beautiful! I thought it was horrible! I tried to explain to him what the smoke stacks really were, and about pollution. But to tell the truth, I liked what he saw better!

A few months later, I began writing about a little girl who starts out saying that because she is "small" there are so many things she cannot do. By the end of the book she realizes that even if she is small she can think big!

My son and other children were the inspiration for the book **I Am Small**, but it also says many of the things I thought about when I was little. It is a quiet book compared to the zing and zap of Mabel Murple's world. Small is more of a dreamer and thinker than a doer. There are many feelings inside one person! A writer can create as many different characters as there are people. A writer can also show us how one person has many different characters inside them — a child can be like a wise old man. When it comes to thinking fresh thoughts, there is no age limit!

Get a mirror and hold it out flat in front of you, as if it was a book you were reading. Walk around the house looking into it — it will be like walking on the ceiling. Be careful — it can make you dizzy!

Start your own "Quote-book" notebook. When you come across a neat saying or expression that you read or hear, copy it down.

When an Elephant Comes to Visit

Sometimes a poem can come in a flash!

I was asked to do a book on children's rights by Unicef, an organization I have often worked with. I thanked them for asking me but said that my style of writing — which is filled with nonsense — did not seem to go with something as serious as children's rights. Perhaps they should look for another writer. They said, "Please think about it." I did research, I read about children's rights. I asked people what they knew. I realized I knew very little about the issue of children's rights and I discovered I was not alone. This made me think that maybe a book would be a good idea. Still, I didn't think I was the one to write it.

• • •

I am in my writing room working on a letter to Unicef. I am trying to find the words to tell them that I haven't found a way to write the book they want on the rights of children. But something starts happening.

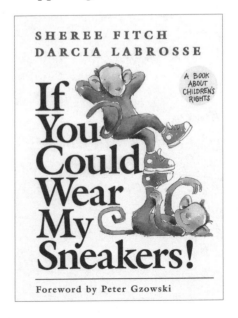

I have the strangest feeling. I reach for another piece of paper and begin writing, fast and furious. Something about an elephant! This is weird, I'm not even thinking and this poem is coming and coming. It's like a little elephant comes and whispers in my ear. It says, "Here, Sheree, take down my poem." It's as if the poem is writing itself. Finally, I stop. Whew!

I read what I have written. Wow! It's a poem about an elephant, all right. An elephant who wants to say what he has to say. A elephant who wants to live in a world of peace.

The whole experience is something magical and part of the mystery that writing can be.

The Eloquent Young Elephant

Did you hear the elephants
Trumpeting last night?
They thundered past my bedroom
The earth rumbled back in fright

They were going to fight a battle
Thump-galumphing off to war
Did you hear a wee small voice say
"What are we fighting for?"

...

Pretend you are an animal who has something to complain about! Think about what you would say.

"The Eloquent Young Elephant" was one of the very few poems that came in a burst and was almost perfect the first draft! All my other writing takes rewriting and rewriting and rewriting again. The title poem of the collection — "If You Could Wear My Sneakers" — was first published in a magazine and I changed it at least ten times before I got the final version. Another poem, "The Beagle and the Beluga and the Eagle's Fine Times," was a final version of one I'd started seven years before the writing of the book (when we had a beagle dog who loved bagels!).

The book **If You Could Wear My Sneakers** contains nonsense poems connected to fifteen of the rights of children declared by the United Nations Convention on the Rights of the Child. Sometimes I am asked this question: Of the books you have written, which is your favorite? I usually say that it's the one I will write tomorrow! But the Sneakers book does have a special meaning to me. I hope that, after reading the book, children and adults will talk about what rights really mean. (For example, we do have a right to express our opinion, but we don't have the right to hurt someone else by what we say.) I hope that underneath the fun of the poetry, readers will think about how we sometimes need to "wear each other's sneakers," to understand our differences and our sameness. It is a very, very special book to me.

Read about a person whose life has been inspiring: Florence Nightingale, Mother Teresa, Martin Luther King, etc.

A year after the elephant invited itself in and told me the poem, I was in Africa and went on safari. I saw a real baby elephant for the first time ever. It was awesome. "Thank-you," I whispered to him as he looked me right in the eye. "Thank-you for helping me write about rights."

I will always remember reading the story of Harriet Tubman and how she worked for the Underground Railroad to help free her people from slavery. She was a fighter for rights! It was a story that changed how I looked at the world when I was in elementary school. In recent years, **Naomi's Road** by Joy Kogawa has had the same effect on me. So has **Uncle Ronald** by Brian Doyle. Although they are fiction, they are examples of situations in which young people have found themselves — situations that have demanded strength, action, and faith in the face of hardship and sadness. These books made me realize there were real people with such courage — heroes do exist!

Of Mice & Mothers

WOW!

There is a lot of writing energy in anger.

I have climbed an iceberg in the Arctic, and a mountain in the country of Bhutan. I have been on safari in Africa, with lions right nearby. All of these wonderful trips have come about because of my writing. The little girl who read books and dreamed of traveling to far-off places grew up to have some wonderful real-life adventures. I would like to say I'm not afraid of anything. But…I am. I'm especially afraid of

mice. Almost every house we've lived in, we've had mice! Every time, I yell and jump on the bed, and the boys chase the mouse away. They got used to them, but I never did.

Tell a story as if your life depends on it.

• • •

Finally! We have moved into a home with no mice! "I want to celebrate!" I say to my boys.

I spoke too soon! A mouse pops out as if to say "welcome!" I can't believe this! There's a mouse in this house, too! I rant. I rave. I am furious to think I have to share my house with them once again!

Finally, Dustin, tired of my complaining says, "Mum, why don't you just write about it? There's a mouse in my house. It rhymes, you know. You always feel better when you write!"

Harumph! I think. But… he's right. It does sound like the beginning of a poem. I start the poem and it takes off like it's on fire! I am making myself laugh as I write, too!

At the end of the book **There's a Mouse in My House**, the boy and the mouse are friends and they discover a world of storytelling together. I started off thinking that I was the mother in the book, and I ended up realizing I was also the mouse!

Am I still frightened by mice? Yes! Writing the book didn't make me get over my fear, but it helped me admit my fear. Writing like a maniac in a fury helped me get rid of the anger and even laugh at myself. What is more amazing to me is how many people have great stories about mice!

I know this poem by heart and it is my one of my favorites to "tell" because there is dialogue between different voices and lots of drama. As I was writing it, I didn't know how it would end. I didn't know that I would actually feel sorry for the mouse when she told her life story. Until the very end of writing the story, I did not know the mouse's name was Sheherazade, just like the storyteller in Arabian Nights who must tell stories to save her life. There are so many things that come into your stories once you have opened the door to your imagination. Dustin was right, I always feel better when I write! It's an adventure waiting to happen and you don't have to know what's going to happen before you start. Just let it roll!

You can rage on the page and turn it into something fun.

You can even put yourself in a story!

Worlds We Know and Love

On a school visit, a boy asked "Are you magic?" I didn't know how to answer. Finally, I stammered out, "Um, yes, in a way. And so are you! So is everyone." He seemed happy with that answer. But...sometimes, I just don't get it!

•   •   •

I'm talking to a school group, and it's question-and-answer time. A young boy puts up his hand and says, "I like your poems, but when are you going to write a real book?"

Everybody laughs. At first, I don't know what he means. "But...but...they *are* real books," I stammer.

"No, a *real* book, " he continues, "like R. L. Stine! I mean a chapter book! A scary one!"

"Is that your favorite kind of book?" I ask.

"Uhuh!" he nods, excited.

"Well, maybe I could do a chapter book," I agree. "Maybe. But I'd have to do one like I would like to do. After all, I'm not R. L. Stine. I don't think I'd be very good at scary."

"Why?"

"Because I think I'd get too scared." Everybody laughs.

"How about a funny chapter book?" someone else suggests. Funny? Well maybe I would try funny!

"I still like scary best," says the boy.

"That's okay," I say. But the boy has more to say.

"R. L. Stine has a lot more books than you!" he says.

"I know," I say. "I'm actually a very slow writer."

"And...he makes a lot of money, too, and," the boy smiles at me with encouragement, "maybe you could too if you did a scary chapter book."

"Maybe *you* should try someday, eh?" I ask him.

He shakes his head back and forth — no. "No. I'm going to be a detective when I grow up," he says.

"Wow," I say. I think of my sister, the police officer. People are all so different!

Not everyone will like everything you write.

Today, notice people's differences: what they wear, how they eat and walk, the sound of their voices, and even what they smell like.

That boy reminded me of something very important to a writing maniac — to keep challenging myself! I had just finished writing a play, only the second one I had ever written. It was a real learning experience — like rubbing your head and patting your tummy at the same time. Even though I had written various kinds of things — poems for adults, essays, articles, scripts and screenplays for radio and television — and even though I hoped each one of my poetry books was different from the last one, I had never thought about a chapter book.

I went home that day and thought about what he had said and what his classmates suggested. A funny chapter book. Could I? If I did, what would I write about? I would write about a school just like his, I thought, a small school that seems like a big family. I have gone into so many schools in my life, and it is a world I know and love. I knew the setting for the story would be important in a chapter book. If I used my imagination and found the right situation, maybe it would work. That's when the ideas for **The Hullabaloo Bugaboo Day** and **The Other Author Arthur** began. As you can tell from the titles I chose, I wanted a book that still played with words and language.

Above all else, the boy reminded me just how many kinds of readers there are. Some people read fast, some people read slow. Faster does not equal smarter. Some people like poetry. Some would rather read about science or history. Some people would rather paint than read or write at all. Or they would rather shoot basketballs. Or dance.

Readers are people. Like snowflakes, no two are alike.

Ask people about what they like to read.

Think about the worlds you know and love best. Some examples: the basketball court, going to music practice, baby-sitting your brother or sister, your classroom, your grandmother's house.

Mushy Stuff

Simple does not equal easy!

One morning, not too long before Valentine's Day, I woke up and looked at my husband. I thought: I would like to write him a love poem instead of buying him a card.

. . .

I slip quietly down the stairs, into my writing room. I go to work. I think: how can I say I love him without using the words I love you? What would I give him, if I could? That's the question I start out with and, to answer it, I write *If I were the moon, I'd shine down my light*..... And I keep on going.

I realize that what I am writing is about more than just how I feel about my husband. It is like a lullaby. It is a love poem for my husband, yes, but also for all the people I love. It is something I wish for my parents, my friends, my grandparents, my sister and brother, even people I have met once and never seen again. I wish it for people who are no longer living, whose memory I still cherish. It is about being together, and also about being together even when you are apart.

For a very short and simple poem that means so much, it takes me a lot of time before I am happy with every word.

Today go outside: smell the air; look at the ground for five minutes, and at the clouds; touch ten different objects; swing on a swing; study the shape of a flower or a tree.

Maybe you are saying, "Yuck! Love poems — give me a break!" Well, what if I said to you that maybe everything you write is a sort of love letter to the world? A way of celebrating life and facing challenges and expressing your feelings and thinking deeply? A way to connect and communicate with others?

Just asking.

Maybe — just maybe — that is what makes us want to write.

P.S. I hope you do write a love letter to someone for real someday.

Stay inside: listen to voices, music, noise; look for five shades of pink; name as many shapes as you can; sit very still; listen to your breath. Remember, you are always writing!

Writing is important, but so is your whole life!

THE WRITE STUFF

- Write what it's like when you wake up at night in the dark. (Remember use your five senses!)

- Make a list of fears you have. Write about one of them.

- Search for a line written by another writer that inspires you. Use it in your story. (Remember to tell where you got it from!)

- Create a character who is afraid of something silly — like pink and purple polka dots. Write a story about how the character overcomes this fear.

- Write about three things, trying to use their motion and energy in the word music of the poem. Topic suggestions: a rocking chair, a train, a swing, a motorboat.

- Start seeing things you don't like as "good" things to write about. Some examples: eating liver, itchy sweaters, the measles, having to speak in front of people.

- Write a story with a surprise ending.

- Write a shaped poem by tracing your hand. Around the outline print words that describe things hands do. Next, make a poem in the shape of a star, an octopus, a tree.

- Write a different ending to a story you read.

- Write a Word Song, which is a poem that uses lots of sound effects in it. Try *kaboom*! Try *crash* and *splash*! Try *clickety clickety clickety clack*!

- Ask a *what if* question and begin writing. Your answer could be a story.

- Write a letter to a character you met in a book.

- Get pictures of yourself when you were small and make a poster. Write about being little (using all your senses) and glue the writing on the poster.

- Write for five minutes using this opening for your first sentence: In my Topsy-Turvy World, fish fly and birds swim and …

- Do research on an issue in the world you're interested in. Some examples: the environment, poverty, saving whales. Write about it as a reporter. Now write about it as a fiction writer. Now write about it as a poet.

- Take two words and play with them.

  Example: beagle and bagel
              kitchen and kittens
              llamas and pajamas

- Write a poem (without rhyme) called "Heroes."

- Write down five things that make you furious. Write about one and see where you end up!

- List five verbs that describe eating. Some examples: munching, chewing. Now list verbs that describe walking, crying, laughing.

- Write a conversation between three people.

- Write the first chapter for a chapter book.

- Write a love letter to your pet.

Dear Reader:

I got up this morning and did my stretches and sit-ups. I ate breakfast and wrote. I answered phone calls. I wrote. I did laundry. I wrote. I read. I went for a walk. I ate. I wrote. I started supper. I'm writing again. It's a perfect day for me! Some days, I can only write a few lines before I fall asleep. Even on the days I am on the road, I try to write something.

I looked at my first notes for this book — April 9, 1997! More than three years ago! In that time, I learned what it's like to write about real things that have happened to me. I think it has been the hardest thing to write, ever! Over the three years, I have written other books and two plays. I have traveled. I have lived my life. I have been researching and making notes for several years. Now, I am getting ready to start my first novel. It's as exciting as that first poem when I was in grade two.

At the beginning of this book, on page 7, is a poem I wrote especially for you, someone who might be asking questions like these: Who is a writer? How do I become a writer? What does a writer do? Now that you've read how I became a writing maniac, maybe you can see the answers to some of those questions in the poem.

You are a writer when you write. Maybe you will publish something someday. Maybe you won't want to, but will keep your writing as something private.

Whatever dream you dream, dear reader, I wish you well. I might not know your name, but I think I know a little about you. If you read this book, just maybe you think and dream and care and wonder a lot like I do.

And maybe you read and read and read and write and write and write!

And maybe, just maybe, you're a bit of a writing maniac, yourself!

Love,
Sheree

So, What's a Meta-phor?
A List of Writing Words

Writing maniacs learn early that learning about writing never ends: you *do* have to know the rules before you break the rules! If you waited until you knew them all, you'd never begin writing, but you can learn as you go, too. To help you get started, I've made a list of some terms I've used in this book and what they mean. You might know most of them already, but it never hurts to review some basics.

Add to this list yourself. Ask librarians, teachers, and other writing maniacs if you don't understand. Also, check out books on writing.

I found that writing definitions in your own words and making up your own examples is a really good way to keep these things in your brain forever. Go, maniac, go!

Characters, *page 43*
The individuals in a story, play, poem, etc. Characters are usually people — but not always.

Dialogue, *page 63*
When characters speak to each other. When characters speak to themselves, it's called a monologue.

Drama, *page 63*
Exciting or emotional events. Drama can also be another word for a play, especially when it's on radio or television.

FIGURES OF SPEECH, *page 21*

You've heard of light effects and special effects? Figures of speech are word effects!

Alliteration, *page 21*
When the sounds at the beginning of the words are the same. Look at the first four lines of this poem by Samuel Taylor Coleridge. It's one of my favorites to say out loud because of the alliteration:

> *In Xanadu did Kubla Khan*
> *A stately pleasure-dome decree*
> *Where Alph, the sacred river, ran*
> *In caverns measureless to man*
> *Down to a sunless sea*

Consonance, *page 21*
A kind of rhyme where the vowel sounds are different and the sounds of *consonants* are the same. Consonants are all the letters of the alphabet that aren't vowels (see **rhyme**). Examples of consonance would be *chitter and chatter* or *reader and rider* or *spoon and spin.*

Imagery, *page 21*
Making a picture with words. It's almost as if the writer hands you a word snapshot. You see the picture clearly because an image gives you sharp specific details, not just a general wide-shot view. An image sometimes uses *metaphor* and *simile* to make the image, but not always.

> The child huddled in the corner, like a
> frightened puppy.
> We traveled past burnt fields of sad and twisted trees.
> Everything was the color of crumbled ashes.

Metaphor, *page 21*
Cat and fog, remember? A metaphor compares, contrasts, *connects* two or more things without the use of the words *like* or *as* (see *simile*).

> My brain is an old wad of gum.
> Her red nose reminded me of Rudolph the Reindeer's.

Onomatopoeia, *page 21*
The use of a word that sounds like what it means. Words like *ping-pong, zoom, whisper, crash, buzzzzzzz!*

Simile, *page 21*
A comparison or contrast that makes a connection between two things by using the words *like* or *as*.

> My brain is like an old wad of gum.
> Her nose was as red as Rudolph the Reindeer's.

Tongue-twister, *page 22*
A sentence or poem that uses *alliteration* for a humorous effect. *She sells seashells by the sea shore* and *Peter Piper picked a peck of pickled peppers* are famous examples.

Article, *page 65*

A type of *essay* found in a newspaper or magazine.

Essay, *page 65*

Not just a homework assignment! An essay is a piece of writing of a certain length on a certain *topic* or subject meant to inform or convince or make a reader think. It often involves some *research* and careful arrangement of the facts. A good essay is clear and presents the facts in a way that makes sense. I think good essays are works of art! Often, the best essays are also the most creative as well.

Legend, *page 43*

A story that's been told over and over, and has traveled from one generation to the next through storytelling or "word of mouth." Legends often contain elements of magic and the supernatural, and were meant to offer an explanation of how things got to be the way they are or, sometimes, to teach.

   Different cultures have different legends to answer questions and express their beliefs. Like how did the moon get in the sky? Or what are stars? Michael Kusugak's, *Northern Lights, The Soccer Trails* tells an Inuit legend.

Myth, *page 43*

A story that's been told over and over, and has traveled from one generation to the next through storytelling or "word of mouth." Like *legends*, myths are stories people have been telling each other for centuries to explain the world to themselves, but myths deal with the world of gods and goddesses, and the events that happened to them. Even though different parts of the world have different mythologies, it's amazing how the messages or themes in the myths are often the same. Myths of loss and recovery, of how things began, of greed and sacrifice, of bravery and cowardice, for example, can be found in most mythologies.

Play, *page 17*
Shakespeare wrote them! A play is just another way to tell a story. Instead of the page, a play is a story written for the stage. It's performed by *actors* (the characters in the story) in front of a theater audience.

Script (screenplay), *page 65*
A piece of writing that will be delivered to an audience. A news announcer reads a script to tell the news. An actor learns a script in order to act in a film or on stage. A finished play is called a *playscript* or maybe *radio script*. A finished film script is called the *screenplay*. When you write **dialogue** for your characters, you can say you have "scripted" their lines. Script can also mean a body of writing. A finished book (before it's published) is a *manuscript*. And now I have no more script on script! Whew!

Story, *page 15*
Funny or sad, serious or mysterious, every story has a beginning, a middle, and an ending. Every story has one or more **characters**. In every story, things happen; that's the *action*. Action and events make up the *plot* of the story. Where the story takes place is called the *setting*. When you have finished reading a good story, you'll see that some change has taken place. It doesn't have to be a big change, like moving to a desert island. Often, it's simply that a character learns something new. Almost always, the character has to face a problem or an obstacle in the story. This is called the *conflict* and provides the **drama** in the story. At some point in the story all the events lead up to an important deciding moment for the character. That's called the *climax*. After that, the story winds down toward the finish and the winding down is called the *denouement*.

   After reading a great story, I look at the world and what happens in it in a new and different way. In stories I like best, I care about the characters and what happens to them. If I think about it, I've learned something too. Everyone has stories to tell. If you think of writing as "talking a story on paper," it's a good way to begin.

We use language in certain ways so others can understand us when we speak or write. A sentence is a sentence because of the way we use *parts of speech*. If you only had **nouns** in a sentence it would not be a sentence.

> Boy apple classroom.

This is not a sentence because it makes no sense! Other *parts of speech* are needed.

Noun, *page 52*
The word for a person, place, or thing.

> The boy ate apples in the kitchen.

Boy, apples, kitchen — these are nouns because they refer to a person, a thing, and a place.

Pronoun, *page 52*
A word used instead of a noun.

> He ate them in the kitchen.

He and *them* are pronouns in this sentence: *he* is used instead of the boy; *them* is used instead of apples. Other pronouns: *I, you, us, we, they, she, me, it, that, who, which, what.*

Adjective, *page 52*
A word that describes a noun.

> The new boy ate rotten apples in the greasy kitchen.

New, rotten and *greasy* are the adjectives.

Verb, *page 52*

An action word. A verb is like a non-stop battery, a busybody, it's always *doing* something.

> I scrambled eggs.
> You climbed up the hill.
> My father is singing.
> He burped, then said, "Excuse me!"

Scrambled, climbed, is singing, burped, said are all verbs.

Adverb, *page 52*

A word that describes a verb. A good trick for spotting adverbs is to look for words that end in *-ly*.

> I scrambled the eggs carefully.
> You climbed quickly up the hill.
> My father is bravely singing.
> He burped loudly then softly said, "Excuse me!"

Carefully, quickly, bravely, loudly, softly are adverbs.

Poetry happens when words tiptoe, tap-dance, twist or tango off your tongue! Besides "word song," that's my favorite definition of poetry. There's been a lot of them over time — make up one that you like. Here's another: a poem is the expression of the thoughts, feelings, observations, experiences of a poet.

Form
The overall design of the poem. A poet can choose to write in any of the many different forms of poetry that exist. The design includes a pattern of *rhythm* and a *rhyme* scheme. The form or design of a poem also depends upon how long or short the poem is. Different forms have different rules about rhyme, rhythm, and length. You could say they are like recipe instructions for making poems.

Rhythm, *page 17*
The number of beats and pauses in a line of poetry. You hear the rhythm when you read a poem out loud, but you can train yourself to hear the rhythm in a line when you read silently.

Rhyme, *page 17*
When two or more words have the same or almost the same vowel sound (*a, e, i, o, u* and sometimes *y*, and combinations of these vowels) and the other sounds that follow are identical. It's easier if you just remember an example: hay, sleigh, gray. Rhyming words have to sound the same, not be spelled the same. My favorite rhyme I ever discovered was when I rhymed Copenhagen (a city) with station wagon!

FORMS OF POETRY

Although the form of a poem is important, a poet doesn't always follow the rules — a poem doesn't even have to rhyme! But whatever form the poem is in , the poet always chooses and uses language in a particular way.

Ballad, *page 21*
A very old form of poetry that was originally sung to music and told a story. Ballads are still sung in folk songs today and many poets use the form for poetry meant to be read or recited. My favorite ballad of all time is "The Cremation of Sam Magee" by Robert Service.

Concrete poem, *page 52*
Sometimes called a *shaped poem,* a poem more for the eye than the ear. Its letters and words make a shape or design on the page. Here's a part of a shaped poem from *Toes in my Nose:*

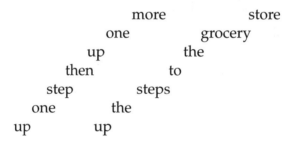

Haiku, *page 21*
A Japanese form of poem that gives an image in a flash. It usually doesn't rhyme, and is composed of three lines of seventeen *syllables* (number of beats in a word): five syllables in the first line, seven syllables in the second line, five syllables in the third line. Here's an example titled "Hide and Seek":

> In the field, a deer.
> I blink once, he disappears
> Overhead, crows laugh.

Nonsense poetry, *page 22*
A verse form that depends more on the sound of words and sounds inside of words than on the meaning. It doesn't have to make sense — no sense, get it? Often nonsense does make a kind of sense in a topsy-turvy way, if that makes any sense! The poem "Jabberwocky" by Lewis Carrol is a famous example of nonsense.

Sonnet, *page 21*
A fixed form of poetry of fourteen lines with a certain rhyme scheme. There are many variations on the sonnet, and the form was old when Shakespeare discovered it. He wrote one of the most famous love sonnets of all: Sonnet 18 by William Shakespeare begins *Shall I compare thee to a summer's day?* I like to practice sonnets using this poem as a model — here's an example titled "Unlove Sonnet to my Selfish Brother":

> Shall I compare thee to a popsicle?
> Your heart is cold and frozen as chipped ice
> Why won't you let me ride your bicycle?
> Who knows? You might enjoy just being nice
> Perhaps you think I'd crash and break your bike
> I promise I'll be careful as you are
> Or maybe you're just doing what you like
> It's just a bike, you jerk, and not a car!
> Next time you ask me if I'll clean your room
> I'll just say no, no matter what you pay
> I'll hand you mop and bucket, brush and broom
> Then steal your bike awhile and ride away
> > But I could never be as cold as you
> > You popsicle! You drip! You, meanie, you!

Read and Read and Read…

If I listed all the books that have affected my life, I'd never have enough paper. That's because I am a reading maniac, as well as a writing maniac! But here's a few titles and authors I love.

Ten Books/Stories that Changed My Life (in the order I think I read them)

The House at Pooh Corner by A.A. Milne
Little Women by Louisa May Alcott
Stories in a children's Bible
The Swiss Family Robinson by Johann David Wyss
The Diary of Anne Frank
The Story of Harriet Tubman
The Bat-Poet by Randall Jarrell
Miss Rumphius by Barbara Cooney
Sarah, Plain and Tall by Patricia McLachlan
The Chance Child by Jill Paton Walsh

Some of my Favorite Canadian Authors and Books

I've used abbreviations to indicate the age groups of readers I think read them most: children's books (CB), literature for young adults (YA), and in between CB and YA (IB). There are lots of great writers all over the world but I am Canadian, eh?

Joyce Barkhouse, *Pit Pony*, IB
Ann Blades, *A Salmon for Simon*, CB
Jo Ellen Bogart, *Jeremiah Learns to Read*, CB

Karleen Bradford, *There Will Be Wolves*, IB/YA
Martha Brooks, *Being with Henry*, YA
Brian Doyle, *Uncle Ronald*, IB/YA
Sarah Ellis, *Back of Beyond*, YA
Phoebe Gilman, *Gillian Jiggs*, CB
Barbara Greenwood
Monica Hughes, *The Other Place*, YA
Linda Granfield, *In Flanders Fields*, IB/YA
Julie Johnston, *Adam and Eve and Pinch-Me*, IB/YA
Joy Kogawa, *Naomi's Road*, IB
Dennis Lee, *Alligator Pie*, CB/IB/YA
Jean Little, *From Anna*, IB
Janet Lunn, *The Root Cellar*, IB/YA
Kevin Major, *Hold Fast*, YA
Tololwa Mollel, *The Orphan Boy*, CB
Lucy Maud Montgomery, *Anne of Green Gables*, IB
Robert Munsch, *The Paper Bag Princess*, CB
Kenneth Oppel, *Sunwing*, IB
Richard Scrimger, *The Nose from Jupiter*, IB
Kathy Stinson, *Red is Best*, CB
Diana Wieler, *Bad Boy*, YA
Budge Wilson, *The Leaving*, YA

For more information on Canadian authors and illustrators, contact The Canadian Children's Book Centre, 40 Orchard View Blvd Toronto, ON M4R 1B9. They have a web page too, at http://www3.sympatico.ca/ccbc/

My favorite book about a favorite teacher: *Thank You, Mr. Falker* by Patricia Polacco.

**Children's Poets Whose Works I'll Read Forever
because you are never too old for nonsense!**

(in random free-verse order)

Mother Goose
& Dennis Lee, William Blake & A.A. Milne
Lewis Carrol, Lois Simmie
Loris Lesynski, Dr. Seuss!
Jack Prelutsky, Edward Lear
Christina Rosetti
Walter de La Mare!
Carl Sandburg
Robert Louis Stevenson
Spike Milligan
Shel Silverstein
Robert Heidbreder & Tim Wynne-Jones
James Reeves, George Swede
Eve Merriam, Sonja Dunn
(and yes the list goes on and on)
Robert Service, David McCord
sean o'huigan and there's more
but lists just make me bored bored bored
I'd rather read a poem instead
Or be a poet whose poems are read.

Books for the Writing Maniac

Finally, every writer needs reference books, because you have to know the rules of writing before you can break them. You will absolutely need a **dictionary** to find out the meanings of words and so you can spell every word in your final drafts correctly. And a really useful book is a **thesaurus** — sounds like a dinosaur! — which is a dictionary of synonyms (words that mean the same) and antonyms (words that mean the opposite). If you want to know more about the things in the glossary in this book, there are lots of **style guides** available that can teach you more about writing; you should be able to find one that is just right for your age and the way you want to write.

...And Write and Write and Write

\
\
\
\
\
\
\
\
\
\
\
\
\
\
\
\
\
\
\
\
\